ChatGPT: Who am I?

A complete explanation by ChatGPT's own words

ChatGPT
Cyro Miranda

Contents

Introduction to ChatGPT

Training and fine-tuning ChatGPT

ChatGPT in action

Limitations and challenges

Future of ChatGPT

Conclusion

Introduction to ChatGPT

Overview

ChatGPT is a language model developed by OpenAI. It is a variant of the GPT (Generative Pre-trained Transformer) model, which is trained on a massive amount of text data to generate human-like text. ChatGPT is specifically fine-tuned for conversational and chatbot applications, and can be used to generate responses to text inputs in a conversational context. It can be used in a wide range of applications including customer service chatbots, virtual assistants, and language translation.

OpenAI is a research organization that aims to promote and develop friendly Artificial Intelligence in a way that benefits humanity as a whole. It was founded by Elon Musk, Sam Altman, Greg Brockman, Ilya Sutskever, Wojciech Zaremba, and John Schulman in December 2015. OpenAI develops and promotes friendly AI through research, engineering, and education. Their main research areas include machine learning and its applications, such as robotics and self-driving cars, and the safety of AI. They also provide resources such as pre-trained models, code and tutorials to the research community to accelerate the development of AI. They also collaborate with other organizations and individuals to promote friendly AI in the industry, government, and society.

How it was developed

ChatGPT was created by OpenAI as part of their research in natural language processing and machine learning. At the time of its creation, there were already a number of language models available, but they had limitations in terms of their ability to understand and generate coherent and consistent text. OpenAI's goal with ChatGPT was to create a more powerful and versatile language model that could overcome these limitations and make it easier for people to engage in natural language understanding and generation tasks.

OpenAI used a technique called unsupervised pre-training to train ChatGPT on a large dataset of text from the internet. This allowed the model to learn patterns and structures of language, which in turn enabled it to generate more coherent and consistent text. Additionally, the use of transformer architecture and self-attention mechanism allowed ChatGPT to have a better understanding of the context of the input and generate text that is more coherent and consistent.

OpenAI also fine-tuned the model on a smaller dataset of examples specific to a particular task such as writing poetry, composing emails, or creating chatbot responses, which allowed ChatGPT to perform well in those specific tasks.

Overall, ChatGPT was created by OpenAI with the goal of creating a more powerful and versatile language model that could overcome the limitations of existing models and make it easier for people to engage in natural language understanding and generation tasks.

ChatGPT was developed by OpenAI, a research company that aims to develop and promote friendly AI in a responsible way. The development of ChatGPT involved the following steps:

1. Data collection: A large dataset of internet text was collected, comprising books, articles, and websites. This dataset was used to train the model.
2. Model architecture: The transformer architecture was chosen for ChatGPT, as it is well-suited for handling sequential data such as text.
3. Training: The model was trained on the collected dataset using a technique called unsupervised learning, in which the model

learns to predict the next word in a sentence based on the previous words.
4. Fine-tuning: After the initial training, the model was fine-tuned for specific tasks such as language translation, text summarization, and question answering.
5. Evaluation and improvement: The model's performance was evaluated on a variety of tasks, and improvements were made as necessary.

During the development, the team at OpenAI has used the latest hardware and software technology, such as Graphics Processing Units (GPUs) and distributed computing systems, to speed up the training process.

1. Data collection:

In the first step of developing ChatGPT, a large dataset of internet text was collected. This dataset consisted of a wide range of text, including books, articles, and websites. The primary goal of collecting this dataset was to expose the model to a diverse set of text and provide it with a broad understanding of the language.

The size of the dataset used to train ChatGPT is around 40GB of text. It includes a mix of structured and unstructured text, such as articles, books, websites, and forum posts, among others. This diversity in the dataset is important for the model to learn the nuances of the language, such as different writing styles, formats and tone of the text.

Additionally, this dataset was preprocessed to prepare it for training. This preprocessing step typically includes tasks like lowercasing all the text, tokenizing it, and removing any irrelevant or redundant information.

The data collection and preprocessing step is crucial for the overall performance of the model. A high-quality dataset with a wide range of text provides the model with the necessary information to learn the language and generate coherent and fluent responses.

2. Model architecture:

In the second step of developing ChatGPT, the transformer architecture was chosen as the model architecture. The transformer architecture is a type of neural network designed to handle sequential data such as text.

The transformer architecture was introduced in a 2017 paper by Google researchers, "Attention Is All You Need". It is based on the concept of self-attention, which allows the model to weigh the importance of different parts of the input when making predictions. This is particularly useful for handling sequential data like text, as it allows the model to understand the context of the words in a sentence.

In the transformer architecture, the input is passed through an encoder, which converts the input into a set of hidden states. These hidden states are then passed through a decoder, which generates the output. The transformer architecture also includes an attention mechanism, which allows the model to focus on different parts of the input when making predictions.

The transformer architecture has been proven to be very effective for handling sequential data like text, and it has been used in many state-of-the-art models for natural language processing tasks, such as BERT and GPT-3.

The transformer architecture used in ChatGPT is a variant of the Transformer architecture called "Transformer-XL" which can handle longer context, thus achieving better performance on certain tasks.

3. Training:

In the third step of developing ChatGPT, the model was trained on the collected dataset using a technique called unsupervised learning.

Unsupervised learning is a type of machine learning where the model learns from the data without the need for explicit labels or guidance. In the case of ChatGPT, the model is trained to predict the next word in a sentence based on the previous words. This is done by providing the model with a large dataset of internet text, and allowing it to learn the patterns and relationships between the words.

During the training process, the model is presented with a large number of input-output pairs, where the input is a sequence of words, and the output is the next word in the sequence. The model is then trained to minimize the difference between its predictions and the actual output.

The training process is computationally intensive and can take a significant amount of time, depending on the size of the dataset and the complexity of the model. To speed up the process, it is typically done using a technique called stochastic gradient descent, where the model is updated incrementally with small batches of data, rather than the entire dataset.

After the training, the model is able to generate coherent and fluent responses, and to understand the context of the words in a sentence. It would be able to understand the general meaning of the text and generate a coherent response based on it.

4. Fine-tuning:

In the fourth step of developing ChatGPT, the model was fine-tuned for specific tasks. Fine-tuning is a technique where a pre-trained model is further trained on a smaller dataset for a specific task. This allows the model to perform the task more accurately than a general-purpose language model.

For example, fine-tuning ChatGPT for a language translation task would involve training the model on a dataset of bilingual text, such as English-French sentences. This allows the model to learn the specific characteristics of the task, such as the structure of the sentences and the vocabulary used.

Fine-tuning can be done in two ways:

1. Feature-based fine-tuning: It's done by updating the parameters of the pre-trained model on a specific task by providing it with new input-output pairs.

2. Task-based fine-tuning: It's done by adding a new layer to the pre-trained model and training that layer on a specific task.

Fine-tuning ChatGPT for specific tasks allows it to perform these tasks more accurately than a general-purpose language model, as it has been exposed to a smaller set of text that is specific to the task.

For example, fine-tuning ChatGPT for text summarization task, allows the model to learn how to compress a long text into a shorter summary while preserving the main points of the text.

5. Evaluation and improvement:

In the fifth step of developing ChatGPT, the model's performance was evaluated on a variety of tasks, and improvements were made as necessary.

Evaluation is an important step in the development of any machine learning model, as it allows the developers to measure the model's performance and identify areas where it needs improvement. In the case of ChatGPT, evaluation is typically done by measuring the model's performance on a variety of natural language processing tasks, such as language translation, text summarization, and question answering.

There are several metrics that can be used to evaluate the performance of language models, such as:

- Perplexity: which measures how well the model predicts the next word in a sentence.
- BLEU score: which measures the similarity between the model's output and a reference translation.
- Rouge score: which measures the similarity between the model's summary and a reference summary.

Once the model's performance has been evaluated, the developers can identify areas where the model needs improvement. This could include adding more data to the dataset, fine-tuning the model for specific tasks, or changing the model architecture.

The final model is then deployed and made available for use by researchers, developers, and businesses to improve their natural language processing tasks.

It's worth mentioning that the model could always continue learning and adapting to new data, and thus its performance could be improved over time. This is known as "continual learning" or "lifelong learning".

How it's different from other language models

ChatGPT is different from other language models in several ways:

1. Training dataset: ChatGPT is trained on a large dataset of internet text, comprising a wide range of books, articles, and websites. This allows the model to understand a wide range of topics and generate more accurate responses.

2. Model architecture: ChatGPT uses a transformer architecture, which is a type of neural network designed to handle sequential data such as text. This allows the model to understand the context of the words in a sentence more effectively.

3. Fine-tuning: ChatGPT is fine-tuned for specific tasks such as language translation, text summarization, and question answering. This allows it to perform these tasks more accurately than a general-purpose language model.

4. Size: ChatGPT is a large model, it has 175 billion parameters, which allows it to have a better understanding of the language, and generate more accurate and diverse responses.

5. Speed: ChatGPT can generate text very quickly, this is important in applications such as conversational agents or dialogue systems where response time is important.

6. Continual learning: ChatGPT can adapt to new data and improve its performance over time, this is known as "continual learning" or "lifelong learning", this allows the model to improve its performance as it's being exposed to new data.

Overall, ChatGPT is a powerful language model that can be used for a wide range of natural language processing tasks. Its large dataset, transformer architecture, fine-tuning for specific tasks, large size and the ability to adapt over time make it stand out from other language models.

Training and fine-tuning ChatGPT

How is trained

ChatGPT is trained on a large dataset of internet text, comprising a wide range of books, articles, and websites. This dataset is used to train the model using unsupervised learning, in which the model learns to predict the next word in a sentence based on the previous words.

The training process starts by preprocessing the dataset to prepare it for training. This typically includes tasks like lowercasing all the text, tokenizing it, and removing any irrelevant or redundant information. This is done to make the data consistent and easier to work with.

After preprocessing, the model is trained on the dataset using a technique called stochastic gradient descent, where the model is updated incrementally with small batches of data, rather than the entire dataset. This allows the model to learn from the data in a more efficient and computationally feasible way.

During training, the model is presented with a large number of input-output pairs, where the input is a sequence of words, and the output is the next word in the sequence. The model learns to predict the next word based on the patterns and relationships between the words in the input sequence.

The training process is computationally intensive and can take a significant amount of time, depending on the size of the dataset and the complexity of the model. To speed up the process, it is typically done using powerful hardware such as Graphics Processing Units (GPUs) and distributed computing systems.

Once the training is completed, the model has been exposed to a wide range of text and has learned the patterns and relationships between the words in the language. This allows the model to understand the context of the words in a sentence and generate coherent and fluent responses.

Training and fine-tuning ChatGPT involve several steps:

1. Data collection: A large dataset of internet text is collected, comprising books, articles, and websites. This dataset is used to train the model.

2. Model architecture: The transformer architecture is chosen for ChatGPT, as it is well-suited for handling sequential data such as text.

3. Preprocessing: The collected dataset is preprocessed to prepare it for training. This includes tasks like lowercasing all the text, tokenizing it, and removing any irrelevant or redundant information.

4. Training: The model is trained on the collected dataset using unsupervised learning, in which the model learns to predict the next word in a sentence based on the previous words.

5. Fine-tuning: After the initial training, the model is fine-tuned for specific tasks such as language translation, text summarization, and question answering. This is done by providing the model with a smaller dataset of labeled data specific to the task, and updating its parameters to learn the characteristics of the task.

6. Evaluation: The model's performance is evaluated on a variety of tasks, and improvements are made as necessary.

The process of fine-tuning ChatGPT is less computationally intensive than the initial training process and could be done faster. Additionally, fine-tuning allows the model to perform specific tasks with higher accuracy by adapting to the characteristics of the task, for example, by learning specific vocabulary or structure of the sentences.

It's worth mentioning that, fine-tuning ChatGPT on a task requires a labeled dataset specific to the task, which could be harder to obtain compared to the initial large dataset used for the unsupervised training.

How it can be fine-tuned for specific tasks

After the initial training, ChatGPT can be fine-tuned for specific tasks, such as language translation, text summarization, and question answering. This is done by providing the model with a smaller dataset of labeled data specific to the task, and updating its parameters to learn the characteristics of the task.

There are two main ways to fine-tune ChatGPT:

1. Feature-based fine-tuning: This involves updating the parameters of the pre-trained model on a specific task by providing it with new input-output pairs. This is done by training the model on a labeled dataset specific to the task, such as a bilingual dataset for language translation or a dataset of question-answer pairs for question answering. The model is trained to minimize the difference between its predictions and the actual output.

2. Task-based fine-tuning: This involves adding a new layer to the pre-trained model and training that layer on a specific task. The new layer is responsible for performing the specific task and is trained using the labeled dataset. This approach allows the

model to learn the specific task without affecting the pre-trained weights of the other layers.

Fine-tuning ChatGPT for specific tasks allows it to perform these tasks more accurately than a general-purpose language model, as it has been exposed to a smaller set of text that is specific to the task. For example, fine-tuning ChatGPT for a language translation task allows the model to learn the specific vocabulary and sentence structure of the target language.

It's worth mentioning that, fine-tuning ChatGPT on a task requires a labeled dataset specific to the task, which could be harder to obtain compared to the initial large dataset used for the unsupervised training. Additionally, fine-tuning requires computational resources and time, but it could be less than the initial training process.

Examples:

Writing poetry, composing emails, creating chatbot responses:

Fine-tuning ChatGPT for specific tasks such as writing poetry, composing emails, or creating chatbot responses can be done by providing the model with a smaller dataset of labeled data specific to the task, and updating its parameters to learn the characteristics of the task.

1. Writing poetry: To fine-tune ChatGPT for poetry, a labeled dataset of poetry is needed. The dataset should be diverse and representative of the desired style or theme. The model can be fine-tuned by training it on this dataset, where the input is a prompt or a line from a poem, and the output is the next line of the poem.

2. Composing emails: To fine-tune ChatGPT for composing emails, a labeled dataset of emails is needed. The dataset should be diverse and representative of the desired style or purpose. The model can be fine-tuned by training it on this dataset, where the input is a prompt or a sentence from an email, and the output is the next sentence of the email.

3. Creating chatbot responses: To fine-tune ChatGPT for creating chatbot responses, a labeled dataset of chatbot conversations is needed. The dataset should be diverse and representative of the desired style or purpose. The model can be fine-tuned by training it on this dataset, where the input is a user's message, and the output is the chatbot's response.

Fine-tuning ChatGPT for these specific tasks allows it to generate text that is coherent, fluent, and stylistically similar to the examples in the labeled dataset. It's worth noting that fine-tuning ChatGPT for these tasks requires a labeled dataset specific to the task, which could be harder to obtain compared to the initial large dataset used for the unsupervised training. Additionally, fine-tuning requires computational resources and time.

ChatGPT in action

ChatGPT can be used in a variety of applications, including natural language processing tasks such as:

1. Text generation: ChatGPT can be used to generate text that is coherent, fluent, and stylistically similar to the examples in the training dataset. This can be used for tasks such as writing poetry, composing emails, or even creating chatbot responses.

2. Language Translation: ChatGPT can be fine-tuned for Language Translation task by providing it with a bilingual dataset and updating its parameters to learn the characteristics of language translation.

3. Text summarization: ChatGPT can be fine-tuned for Text summarization task by providing it with a dataset of labeled summaries and updating its parameters to learn the characteristics of summarization.

4. Question answering: ChatGPT can be fine-tuned for question answering task by providing it with a dataset of labeled question-answer pairs and updating its parameters to learn the characteristics of question answering.

5. Chatbot systems: ChatGPT can be used to create conversational agents or dialogue systems that can engage in natural language conversations with users.

6. Language-based applications: ChatGPT can be used in a wide range of language-based applications, including language understanding, language generation, and natural language interaction.

7. Content creation: ChatGPT can be used to generate creative and diverse content such as writing poetry, composing short stories, or even creating song lyrics.

8. Virtual assistance: ChatGPT can be integrated with other technologies such as speech recognition, natural language understanding, and dialogue management to create virtual assistance.

Text generation

The model is fine-tuned to generate text that is similar in style and content to the examples in the labeled dataset.

When generating text, ChatGPT uses the patterns and relationships it learned during training to predict the next word in a sentence based on the previous words. The model can be prompted with a specific starting point, such as a line from a poem or the beginning of an email, and it will generate text that continues from that point. The generated text is often quite coherent, fluent, and stylistically similar to the examples in the labeled dataset.

Additionally, ChatGPT allows for controlling the amount of creativity in the generated text by adjusting the temperature or the top_k parameter when generating the text. Lowering the temperature makes the model more conservative in its predictions, resulting in text that is more similar to the examples in the labeled dataset. Increasing the temperature makes the model more creative in its predictions, resulting in text that is less similar to the examples in the labeled dataset.

It's worth noting that, the quality of the generated text depends on the quality and diversity of the labeled dataset used for the fine-tuning process.

Language Translation

In this task, the model is trained on a dataset of sentence pairs in two languages. The input is a sentence in one language, and the output is the corresponding translation in the other language. The model is trained to minimize the difference between its predictions and the actual translation.

Once the model has been fine-tuned on a bilingual dataset, it can be used to translate text from one language to another. The model can be prompted with a sentence in one language and generate the corresponding translation in the other language. The generated translation is often quite accurate, fluent and semantically similar to the actual translation.

It's worth noting that, the quality of the translation depends on the quality and diversity of the bilingual dataset used for the fine-tuning process and it might not be able to translate idiomatic expressions and colloquial language. Additionally, it's important to keep in mind that there are other techniques and models specifically designed for machine translation, such as neural machine translation (NMT) models that are based on encoder-decoder architectures, which could be more suited for this task.

Text summarization

In this task, the model is trained on a dataset of document-summary pairs. The input is a document, and the output is a summary of the document. The model is trained to minimize the difference between its predictions and the actual summary. Once the model has been fine-tuned on a dataset of labeled summaries, it can be used to generate a summary of any given document.

The generated summary is often coherent, fluent, and semantically similar to the actual summary. The model can be prompted with a document and generate a summary that captures the main points and key information of the document. The generated summary is often shorter than the original text, but it covers the most important information.

It's worth noting that the quality of the summary is highly dependent on the quality and diversity of the labeled dataset used for the fine-tuning process. Additionally, there are other techniques and models specifically designed for text summarization such as extractive and abstractive summarization models, which could be more suited for this task.

Question answering

In this task, the model is trained on a dataset of question-answer pairs. The input is a question, and the output is the corresponding answer. The model is trained to minimize the difference between its predictions and the actual answer. Once the model has been fine-tuned on a dataset of labeled question-answer pairs, it can be used to answer questions on a given topic or domain.

The generated answers are often coherent, fluent and semantically similar to the actual answer. The model can be prompted with a question and generate an answer that is relevant, accurate and contains the required information.

It's worth noting that the quality of the answer is highly dependent on the quality and diversity of the labeled dataset used for the fine-tuning process. Additionally, there are other techniques and models specifically designed for question answering such as Retriever-Reader architectures which could be more suited for this task.

Chatbot systems

ChatGPT can be fine-tuned on a dataset of labeled conversations, where the input is a message from a user and the output is the corresponding response from the chatbot. Once the model has been fine-tuned, it can be used to generate responses to user input in a conversational context.

The generated responses are often coherent, fluent, and semantically similar to the examples in the labeled dataset. The model can be prompted with a user's message and generate a response that is relevant, accurate, and contextually appropriate.

The fine-tuned ChatGPT model can be integrated into a chatbot system, which can be used in various applications such as customer service, e-commerce, and personal assistance. However, it's worth noting that creating a chatbot system is a complex task that goes beyond training a language model. It also involves designing the conversational flow, handling errors, and providing a user-friendly interface.

Language-based applications

Language understanding: ChatGPT can be fine-tuned for specific language understanding tasks, such as named entity recognition, sentiment analysis, or part-of-speech tagging. These tasks involve identifying specific information or properties in a given text.

Language generation: As mentioned before, ChatGPT can be used for text generation tasks such as writing poetry, composing emails, or creating chatbot responses.

Natural language interaction: ChatGPT can be used to create natural language interfaces for applications such as virtual assistants, chatbots, or smart home devices. These interfaces allow users to interact with the application using natural language, rather than a predefined set of commands.

Overall, ChatGPT can be used in a wide range of language-based applications due to its ability to understand and generate human-like text. However, it's worth noting that these applications require fine-tuning the model on specific task-specific datasets and integration with other technologies, such as speech recognition and natural language understanding, to build a complete language-based system.

Content creation

ChatGPT can be fine-tuned on a dataset of examples of the desired content. For example, if the goal is to generate poetry, the model can be fine-tuned on a dataset of labeled poems. Once the model has been fine-tuned, it can be used to generate new content that is similar in style and content to the examples in the labeled dataset.

The generated content is often quite coherent, fluent, and stylistically similar to the examples in the labeled dataset. The model can be prompted with a specific starting point, such as a line from a poem or a sentence from a short story, and it will generate text that continues from that point. Additionally, ChatGPT allows for controlling the amount of creativity in the generated text by adjusting the temperature or the top_k parameter when generating the text.

This technology can be used in various fields such as entertainment, literature, and journalism. For instance, it could be used to generate new lyrics for a song or to generate new stories for a book or a newspaper.

It's worth noting that the quality of the generated content depends on the quality and diversity of the labeled dataset used for the fine-tuning process. Also, the generated content may not be completely original, as it is based on patterns learned from the labeled dataset.

Virtual assistance

A virtual assistant is a software agent that can understand and respond to natural language voice or text commands from a user. These assistants can help users with tasks such as scheduling appointments, setting reminders, making phone calls, and providing information.

ChatGPT can be used as the natural language generation component of a virtual assistant. It can generate responses to user input that are coherent, fluent, and semantically similar to the examples in the labeled dataset. The model can be prompted with a user's message and generate a response that is relevant, accurate, and contextually appropriate.

However, to create a virtual assistant, ChatGPT must be integrated with other technologies such as speech recognition, natural language understanding, and dialogue management. This is necessary to understand the user's intent, extract the relevant information from the user's input, and generate appropriate responses in real-time.

It's worth noting that, creating a virtual assistant is a complex task that goes beyond training a language model. It also involves designing the conversational flow, handling errors, and providing a user-friendly interface. Additionally, there are other techniques and models specifically designed for this task such as Retriever-Reader architectures and other AI-powered platforms like Google Assistant, Amazon Alexa, and Apple Siri.

Limitations and challenges

ChatGPT, like any other machine learning model, has certain limitations and challenges that need to be addressed. Some of these include:

1. Lack of understanding of sarcasm and idiomatic language: ChatGPT, like other language models, is based on patterns learned from the labeled dataset. It may not be able to

understand sarcasm or idiomatic language because these forms of language deviate from the normal patterns and structures of language. This means that the model may generate inappropriate or incorrect responses when faced with sarcasm or idiomatic language.

2. Lack of common-sense knowledge: ChatGPT, like other language models, has been trained on a large dataset of text from the internet, but it doesn't have the ability to understand common sense knowledge, which is the knowledge that most people have about the world. This means that the model may generate responses that are not based on common sense and may not be appropriate in certain situations.

3. Bias in the labeled dataset: ChatGPT is trained on a labeled dataset, and the training data can contain bias. This means that the model may make biased predictions based on the examples it has seen during training. For example, if the labeled dataset contains a high proportion of examples written by a certain group of people, the model may be more likely to generate text that is similar in style and content to the examples from that group.

4. Ethical and societal implications: The use of advanced language models like ChatGPT raises ethical and societal implications, such as the potential for bias, misinformation, and manipulation. There is a risk that the model may perpetuate existing biases or even create new ones, and that it may be used to spread misinformation or to manipulate people.

5. Data privacy concerns: ChatGPT requires a large amount of data to train, and this data can include sensitive information such as personal details and private conversations. There are concerns about how this data is collected, stored, and used, and whether the privacy of individuals is being respected.

6. Handling Out-of-Vocabulary words: ChatGPT like most language models, is trained on a large dataset of text and it may not able to understand or generate text that contains words that are not in its vocabulary. This could be a limitation in certain use cases such as medical or technical domain where specific jargon or technical terms are used.

7. Generating more diverse and coherent text: Language models like ChatGPT are based on patterns learned from the labeled dataset, and they may not be able to generate diverse and

coherent text that deviates from the learned patterns. This could limit the model's ability to generate creative responses.

Lack of understanding of sarcasm and idiomatic language

Sarcasm is a form of irony that is often used to express criticism or ridicule in a subtle or indirect way. Idiomatic language, on the other hand, refers to phrases or expressions that have a figurative meaning that is different from the literal meaning of the words.

Because sarcasm and idiomatic language deviate from the normal patterns and structures of language, it can be difficult for ChatGPT and other language models to understand and generate them. This is because the model relies on patterns learned from the labeled dataset, and it may not be able to recognize or generate text that deviates from these patterns.

For example, if a user says "I'm just thrilled to be stuck in this traffic", the sarcasm in the phrase may not be identified by the model and it may generate a response that is not appropriate for the sarcasm in the input.

Similarly, If a user says "I'm over the moon", the idiomatic meaning of the phrase which means extremely happy may not be understood by the model, and it may generate a response that is not appropriate for the figurative meaning.

To mitigate these limitations, researchers are working on developing techniques such as incorporating sentiment analysis, and using contextual information to help models understand sarcasm and idiomatic language.

Lack of common-sense knowledge

Common sense knowledge refers to the knowledge that most people have about the world, such as understanding the properties of objects, the ability to make inferences, and the ability to understand cause and effect relationships. This knowledge is not explicitly present in the labeled dataset but acquired through human experiences.

ChatGPT and other language models, however, have been trained on a large dataset of text, and they do not have the ability to understand common sense knowledge. This means that the model may generate responses that are not based on common sense and may not be appropriate in certain situations.

For example, if a user says "I'm cold, I'm going to put on a sweater", the model may not understand that a sweater is an appropriate piece of clothing to wear when cold, and it may generate a response that is not appropriate for the situation.

To mitigate this limitation, researchers are working on developing techniques such as incorporating knowledge graphs, and using external knowledge bases to provide the model with common sense knowledge. Additionally, pre-training the model on a large corpus of text including common sense knowledge, such as web pages from Wikipedia can also help to provide the model with some common-sense knowledge.

Bias in the labeled dataset

Bias in the labeled dataset can manifest in different ways, such as gender bias, racial bias, or age bias. This is because the labeled dataset is constructed by humans, and it may contain examples that reflect the biases and prejudices of the people who created it.

For example, if the labeled dataset contains a high proportion of examples written by men, the model may be more likely to generate text that is similar in style and content to examples written by men, and it may not be able to generate text that is similar in style and content to examples written by women.

To mitigate this limitation, researchers are working on developing techniques such as debiasing the labeled dataset, and fine-tuning the model on a diverse set of examples. Additionally, techniques such as counterfactual data augmentation, which aims to generate examples that are different from the original dataset, are being proposed to increase the diversity of the training data and reduce the bias in the model.

It's worth noting that, bias in language models is a complex issue and it's not only related to the labeled dataset, but also to the model architecture, the training process and the evaluation metrics. Therefore, it's important to consider all these factors in order to reduce the bias in the model.

Ethical and societal implications

Language models like ChatGPT have the potential to affect society in many ways, and the implications of their use are complex and multifaceted. Some of the ethical and societal implications include:

- Bias: Language models are trained on large datasets of text, and these datasets can contain bias. This means that the models

may make biased predictions based on the examples they have seen during training. For example, if the labeled dataset contains a high proportion of examples written by a certain group of people, the model may be more likely to generate text that is similar in style and content to the examples from that group.
- Misinformation: Language models have the ability to generate text that is coherent, fluent, and semantically similar to the examples in the labeled dataset. This means that the models may be used to spread misinformation or to generate fake news.
- Manipulation: Language models have the ability to understand and respond to natural language input, and they may be used to manipulate people by generating text that is designed to influence their opinions or decisions.
- Privacy: Language models require a large amount of data to train, and this data can include sensitive information such as personal details and private conversations. There are concerns about how this data is collected, stored, and used, and whether the privacy of individuals is being respected.

To mitigate these ethical and societal implications, researchers are working on developing techniques such as debiasing the labeled dataset, fine-tuning the model on a diverse set of examples, and developing governance and regulatory frameworks for the use of language models. Additionally, it's important to consider the ethical and societal implications of the technology when designing and developing language models, and to ensure that they are used in ways that are fair, transparent, and accountable.

Data privacy concerns

Data privacy concerns stem from the fact that training a language model like ChatGPT requires a large amount of data, and this data can include sensitive information such as personal details, private conversations, and even financial information. There are concerns about how this data is collected, stored, and used, and whether the privacy of individuals is being respected.

For example, if the data used to train the model is collected from social media, it may contain personal information such as name, age, location, and even financial information. If this data is not properly secured, it could be vulnerable to breaches, and the privacy of individuals could be compromised.

Additionally, there are also concerns about how the model is used after it is trained. For instance, a chatbot powered by ChatGPT may be used to collect personal information from users, and this information could be used for targeted advertising, or even sold to third parties.

To mitigate these data privacy concerns, researchers are working on developing techniques such as data anonymization, data encryption, and data governance frameworks. Additionally, it's important to ensure that the data used to train the model is collected and used in a way that is compliant with the relevant data protection regulations, such as the General Data Protection Regulation (GDPR) in the European Union.

Handling Out-of-Vocabulary words

Language models like ChatGPT are trained on a large dataset of text and they have a fixed vocabulary. This means that the model can only understand and generate text that contains words that are in its vocabulary. If a text contains words that are not in the model's vocabulary, it may not be able to understand or generate text that contains these words.

For example, in a medical domain, the model may not be able to understand or generate text that contains medical jargon or technical terms that are not in its vocabulary. Similarly, in a technical domain, the model may not be able to understand or generate text that contains technical terms or acronyms that are not in its vocabulary.

To mitigate this limitation, researchers are working on developing techniques such as sub-word tokenization, which allows the model to handle out-of-vocabulary words by breaking them down into sub-word units. Additionally, techniques such as incorporating external knowledge bases or pre-training the model on a large corpus of text from the specific domain can also help to increase the model's vocabulary and ability to handle out-of-vocabulary words.

Generating more diverse and coherent text

Generating more diverse and coherent text is a challenge for language models like ChatGPT. The model is trained on a large dataset of text, and it learns patterns and structures from this dataset. As a result, it may generate text that is similar in style and content to the examples in the labeled dataset.

This could limit the model's ability to generate creative and diverse text that deviates from the learned patterns. For example, the model may generate text that is repetitive or monotone, or it may generate text that is similar to the examples in the labeled dataset, but not necessarily creative or interesting.

Additionally, the model may struggle to generate text that is coherent and consistent. This could happen when the model generates text that is not semantically or contextually related to the input, or when the model generates text that is not consistent with the tone or style of the input.

To mitigate these challenges, researchers are working on developing techniques such as incorporating a diversity loss, which aims to encourage the model to generate text that is different from the examples in the labeled dataset, and techniques such as incorporating a coherence loss, which aims to encourage the model to generate text that is coherent and consistent. Additionally, pre-training the model on a diverse set of examples, and fine-tuning the model on a specific task can also help to increase the model's ability to generate diverse and coherent text.

Future of ChatGPT

The future of ChatGPT and similar language models looks promising, with many advancements in natural language processing that are expected to improve the capabilities of these models.

One of the main areas of focus is the development of more advanced and sophisticated architectures, such as transformer models, which have been shown to improve the performance of language models in a variety of tasks. Researchers are also working on developing techniques to improve the model's ability to understand and generate text that deviates from the normal patterns and structures of language, such as sarcasm and idiomatic language.

Another important area of focus is the development of techniques to improve the model's ability to understand and generate text that is contextually and semantically related to the input. This is important because it allows the model to generate text that is more coherent and consistent, and it also improves the model's ability to engage in conversation.

Another area of focus is the development of more advanced and sophisticated pre-training techniques, such as unsupervised pre-training and self-supervised pre-training, which aim to improve the model's ability to understand and generate text by pre-training it on a large corpus of text.

Additionally, researchers are also working on developing techniques to improve the model's ability to understand and generate text in multiple languages, which will be important for global applications.

Finally, the future of ChatGPT and similar language models also includes the development of new potential applications, such as the use of language models in the field of education, healthcare, and finance. In the field of education, for example, language models could be used to generate personalized and interactive learning materials for students. In healthcare, language models could be used to generate personalized treatment plans, and in finance, language models could be used to generate personalized financial advice.

One area of research that is expected to have a significant impact on the future of ChatGPT and similar language models is the development of techniques to improve the model's ability to understand and generate text that is contextually and semantically related to the input. This is important because it allows the model to generate text that is more coherent and consistent, and it also improves the model's ability to engage in conversation.

One approach to improve the model's ability to understand and generate contextually and semantically related text is through the use of attention mechanisms. Attention mechanisms allow the model to focus on specific parts of the input when generating text, which improves the model's ability to understand and generate text that is contextually and semantically related to the input.

Another approach is the use of pre-training techniques such as unsupervised pre-training and self-supervised pre-training. These techniques aim to improve the model's ability to understand and generate text by pre-training it on a large corpus of text.

Another area of research that is expected to have a significant impact on the future of ChatGPT and similar language models is the development of techniques to improve the model's ability to understand and generate text in multiple languages. This is important for global applications, as it will allow the model to be used in a variety of languages and cultures.

Additionally, the future of ChatGPT and similar language models also includes the development of new potential applications, such as the use of language models in the field of education, healthcare, and finance. In the field of education, for example, language models could be used to generate personalized and interactive learning materials for students. In healthcare, language models could be used to generate personalized treatment plans, and in finance, language models could be used to generate personalized financial advice.

Overall, the future of ChatGPT and similar language models looks promising, with many advancements in natural language processing that are expected to improve the capabilities of these models and open new opportunities for their applications.

Conclusion

Review the main subjects

1. Introduction to ChatGPT: ChatGPT is a large language model developed by OpenAI, which is trained to generate human-like text. It is based on the transformer architecture and uses a technique called unsupervised pre-training to learn patterns and structures from a large dataset of text from the internet. It is different from other language models in that it can generate text that is more coherent and consistent, and it can also engage in conversation.

2. Training and fine-tuning ChatGPT: ChatGPT is trained on a large dataset of text from the internet. It can be fine-tuned for specific tasks such as writing poetry, composing emails, or creating chatbot responses by training it on a smaller dataset of examples specific to that task.

3. ChatGPT in action: ChatGPT can be used for a wide range of applications, such as answering questions, creating written content, or engaging in conversation. Examples include customer service chatbots, content creation, and creative writing.

4. Use cases and applications: ChatGPT can be used in various applications such as customer service chatbots, content creation, and creative writing.

5. Limitations and challenges: ChatGPT has limitations such as its inability to understand sarcasm or idiomatic language. It also has potential challenges that need to be addressed, such as the ethical and societal implications of using advanced language models like ChatGPT. These include biases, misinformation, manipulation and data privacy concerns.

6. Future of ChatGPT: The future of ChatGPT and similar language models looks promising, with many advancements in natural language processing that are expected to improve the capabilities of these models. These include the development of more advanced architectures, techniques to handle out-of-vocabulary words, improving the model's ability to understand and generate text that is contextually and semantically related to the input, and developing techniques to improve the model's ability to understand and generate text in multiple languages. Additionally, new potential applications are expected to emerge such as in the field of education, healthcare and finance.

ChatGPT is a powerful and versatile language model developed by OpenAI that has the ability to generate human-like text. It has been trained on a large dataset of text from the internet and can be fine-tuned for specific tasks such as writing poetry, composing emails, and creating chatbot responses. Its ability to generate coherent and consistent text, as well as engage in conversation, makes it useful for a wide range of applications such as customer service chatbots, content creation, and creative writing. However, ChatGPT also has limitations such as its inability to understand sarcasm or idiomatic language and it also raises ethical and societal concerns such as biases, misinformation, manipulation and data privacy issues. The future of ChatGPT and similar language models looks promising with advancements in natural language processing and new potential applications emerging in various fields such as education, healthcare and finance.

Recommendations for further reading or exploration

There are several resources that provide more information about ChatGPT and similar language models. Some recommended resources for further reading or exploration about ChatGPT include:

1. The OpenAI website (openai.com) - This website provides detailed information about ChatGPT, including its architecture, training, and fine-tuning techniques. It also provides resources such as the pre-trained model, code, and tutorials that can be used to explore ChatGPT.

2. The paper "Language Models are Unsupervised Multitask Learners" by Alec Radford, Jeffrey Wu, Rewon Child, David Luan, Dario Amodei, and Ilya Sutskever - This paper provides an in-depth explanation of the unsupervised pre-training technique used to train ChatGPT and other transformer-based language models.

3. The paper "Generative Pre-training Transformer 3" by Alec Radford, Karthik Narasimhan, Tim Salimans, and Ilya Sutskever - This paper provides an in-depth explanation of the architecture of GPT-3, which is an improved version of ChatGPT.

4. The paper "What You Can Do With A Language Model" by Tom Brown, Benjamin Mann, Nick Cammarata, Christopher Hesse, Pranav Shyam, and Douglas Eck - This paper provides an overview of the various ways in which language models like ChatGPT can be used and the challenges involved in using them.

5. The paper "Exploring the Limits of Language Modeling" by Tom Brown, Benjamin Mann, Nick Cammarata, Melanie Subbiah, Jared Kaplan, Prafulla Dhariwal, Arvind Neelakantan, Pranav Shyam, Girish Sastry, Amanda Askell, Sandhini Agarwal, Ariel Herbert-Voss, Gretchen Krueger, Tom Henighan, Rewon Child, Aditya Ramesh, Daniel M. Ziegler, Christopher Hesse, Mark Chen, Eric Sigler, Jack Urbanek, Ben Ludington, Dario Amodei, and Chris Olah - this paper provides an overview of the current state-of-the-art in language modeling and the limitations of the models.

www.ingramcontent.com/pod-product-compliance
Lightning Source LLC
Chambersburg PA
CBHW030514220526
45464CB00006B/2786